# This is my story. . .

Name: .................................................................................

Date: .................................................................................

# Every Scripture

## Tells a Story

### Devotional Thought Journal
### for Teen Girls

BARBOUR BOOKS
An Imprint of Barbour Publishing, Inc.

ISBN 978-1-68322-860-8

Journal prompts written by JoAnne Simmons.

Published by Barbour Books, an imprint of Barbour Publishing, Inc., 1810 Barbour Drive, Uhrichsville, Ohio 44683, www.barbourbooks.com

*Our mission is to inspire the world with the life-changing message of the Bible.*

Printed in China.

# Introduction

Did you know that God's Word is woven into your very own amazing story? . . . The story of YOU!

Think about it. . .

God created you.

He has specific plans for you.

He gifted you with talents to use for His kingdom.

He sent His One and only Son to die for you.

And, at this very moment, He is preparing a home in heaven for you.

This devotional thought journal features prompts related to specific scripture selections that will help you begin to write out your very own story and see how the Word of God speaks truth and love into your life today (and, in fact, from the very moment God first thought of you!).

While each of the journal sections may not apply to your life *right now*, they certainly may play a part in your future—because God is still busy writing your life adventure. So flip to the sections that interest you the most and begin to record your story—with your hand in God's, He'll be beside you each step of your journey.

Be blessed!

# Contents

Section 1: Here's how my story began . . . . . . . . . . . . . . . . . . . . . . . . .7

Section 2: My name is part of my story. . . . . . . . . . . . . . . . . . . . . . . 13

Section 3: I am wonderfully made . . . . . . . . . . . . . . . . . . . . . . . . . . . 19

Section 4: My faith is the *best* part of my story . . . . . . . . . . . . . . . 31

Section 5: My family is part of my story. . . . . . . . . . . . . . . . . . . . . . .47

Section 6: My friends are part of my story . . . . . . . . . . . . . . . . . . . .75

Section 7: My education is part of my story . . . . . . . . . . . . . . . . . . 89

Section 8: My activities and interests are part of my story . . . . . . . . 115

Section 9: My role models are part of my story . . . . . . . . . . . . . . . .153

Section 10: The places I've lived are part of my story . . . . . . . . . . . . 161

Section 11: My struggles and triumphs are part of my story . . . . . . .169

Section 12: My dreams for marriage and family are part of my story . . . 177

Section 13: God will continue to work in my life for *all* my days . . .189

# Section 1:

Here's how my story began. . .

**Every great story has an epic beginning.**
**And my story is no different. . .**

*You made all the delicate, inner parts of my body*
*and knit me together in my mother's womb.*
*Thank you for making me so wonderfully complex!*
*Your workmanship is marvelous—how well I know it.*
*You watched me as I was being formed in utter seclusion,*
*as I was woven together in the dark of the womb.*
*You saw me before I was born.*
*Every day of my life was recorded in your book.*
*Every moment was laid out*
*before a single day had passed.*

PSALM 139:13–16 NLT

*God* had a plan for me from
the very start of my life.

I was born on ................................................................. .

At this time of day ............................................................. .

In ............................................... (place of birth).

To .............................................. (mother)

and ............................................. (father).

My full given name is ......................................... .

Do you know any details about the day you were born?
Write your birth story here.

........................................................................................

........................................................................................

........................................................................................

........................................................................................

........................................................................................

........................................................................................

........................................................................................

........................................................................................

........................................................................................

........................................................................................

........................................................................................

........................................................................................

........................................................................................

........................................................................................

........................................................................................

........................................................................................

........................................................................................

........................................................................................

........................................................................................

........................................................................................

........................................................................................

Do you have photos and videos of the day you were born?
How does it make you feel when you look at or watch them?

........................................................................................................
........................................................................................................
........................................................................................................
........................................................................................................
........................................................................................................
........................................................................................................
........................................................................................................
........................................................................................................
........................................................................................................
........................................................................................................
........................................................................................................
........................................................................................................
........................................................................................................
........................................................................................................
........................................................................................................
........................................................................................................
........................................................................................................
........................................................................................................
........................................................................................................
........................................................................................................
........................................................................................................

*So give your father and mother joy!*
*May she who gave you birth be happy.*
PROVERBS 23:25 NLT

If you were adopted, share your adoption story here.

*"I will not leave you as orphans;*
*I will come to you."*
JOHN 14:18 ESV

# Section 2:

My name is part of my story.

A good name is to be chosen
rather than great riches,
and favor is better than silver or gold.

**PROVERBS 22:1** ESV

My parents chose my name because

My name means .......................................................................................................

................................................................................................................................ ,

and that inspires me because ...............................................................................

................................................................................................................................

................................................................................................................................

................................................................................................................................

................................................................................................................................

................................................................................................................................

................................................................................................................................

................................................................................................................................

................................................................................................................................

................................................................................................................................

................................................................................................................................

................................................................................................................................

................................................................................................................................

................................................................................................................................

................................................................................................................................

................................................................................................................................

................................................................................................................................

................................................................................................................................

................................................................................................................................

................................................................................................................................

What do you like about your name? If you dislike it,
what would you change it to if you could?

Do you have any nicknames? List each one,
who gave it to you, and how it makes you feel.

# Section 3:

I am wonderfully made.

I praise you because I am fearfully
and wonderfully made; your works are
wonderful, I know that full well.

**PSALM 139:14** NIV

God created me with .................................................................................................. hair,

.................................................................................... eyes, and ...............................................

........................................................................................................................................ .

When I look in the mirror I feel ...................................................................................

...........................................................................................................................................

...........................................................................................................................................

...........................................................................................................................................

...........................................................................................................................................

...........................................................................................................................................

...........................................................................................................................................

...........................................................................................................................................

...........................................................................................................................................

...........................................................................................................................................

...........................................................................................................................................

...........................................................................................................................................

...........................................................................................................................................

...........................................................................................................................................

...........................................................................................................................................

...........................................................................................................................................

...........................................................................................................................................

...........................................................................................................................................

...........................................................................................................................................

*So God created man in his own image, in the image*
*of God he created him; male and female*
*he created them.*
GENESIS 1:27 ESV

21

From my mom, I have inherited these physical features .....................

..............................................................................................

..............................................................................................

and these personality traits ...........................................................

..............................................................................................

..............................................................................................

## What do you most appreciate about these features and traits?

..............................................................................................

..............................................................................................

..............................................................................................

..............................................................................................

..............................................................................................

..............................................................................................

..............................................................................................

..............................................................................................

..............................................................................................

..............................................................................................

..............................................................................................

..............................................................................................

..............................................................................................

..............................................................................................

..............................................................................................

..............................................................................................

..............................................................................................

From my dad, I have inherited these physical features ..............................

..............................................................................................................................

..............................................................................................................................

and these personality traits .............................................................................

..............................................................................................................................

..............................................................................................................................

What do you most appreciate about these features and traits?

..............................................................................................................................

..............................................................................................................................

..............................................................................................................................

..............................................................................................................................

..............................................................................................................................

..............................................................................................................................

..............................................................................................................................

..............................................................................................................................

..............................................................................................................................

..............................................................................................................................

..............................................................................................................................

..............................................................................................................................

..............................................................................................................................

..............................................................................................................................

..............................................................................................................................

..............................................................................................................................

..............................................................................................................................

..............................................................................................................................

What personality traits of yours stand out and
are different from those of your parents?

.......................................................................................................

.......................................................................................................

.......................................................................................................

.......................................................................................................

.......................................................................................................

.......................................................................................................

.......................................................................................................

.......................................................................................................

.......................................................................................................

.......................................................................................................

.......................................................................................................

.......................................................................................................

.......................................................................................................

.......................................................................................................

.......................................................................................................

.......................................................................................................

.......................................................................................................

*"The LORD doesn't see things the way you
see them. People judge by outward
appearance, but the LORD
looks at the heart."*
1 SAMUEL 16:7 NLT

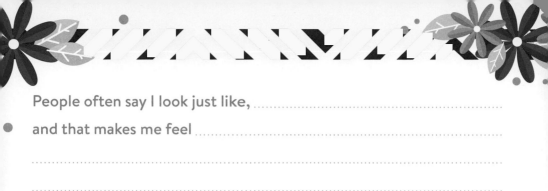

People often say I look just like, ............................................................

and that makes me feel ............................................................

............................................................

............................................................

............................................................

............................................................

............................................................

............................................................

............................................................

............................................................

............................................................

People often say I act just like, ............................................................

and that makes me feel ............................................................

............................................................

............................................................

............................................................

............................................................

............................................................

............................................................

............................................................

............................................................

............................................................

............................................................

............................................................

............................................................

............................................................

Do you believe that you are fearfully
and wonderfully made? Why or why not?
In what ways can you remind yourself of this
fact and celebrate who God made you to be?

**Write a response to the following scripture:**

And yet, O Lord, you are our Father. We are the clay,
and you are the potter. We all are formed by your hand.
Isaiah 64:8 NLT

## What does it mean to be beautiful?

........................................................................................

........................................................................................

........................................................................................

........................................................................................

........................................................................................

........................................................................................

........................................................................................

........................................................................................

........................................................................................

........................................................................................

........................................................................................

........................................................................................

........................................................................................

........................................................................................

........................................................................................

........................................................................................

*Don't be concerned about the outward beauty of
fancy hairstyles, expensive jewelry, or beautiful
clothes. You should clothe yourselves instead with
the beauty that comes from within, the unfading
beauty of a gentle and quiet spirit,
which is so precious to God.*
1 PETER 3:3–4 NLT

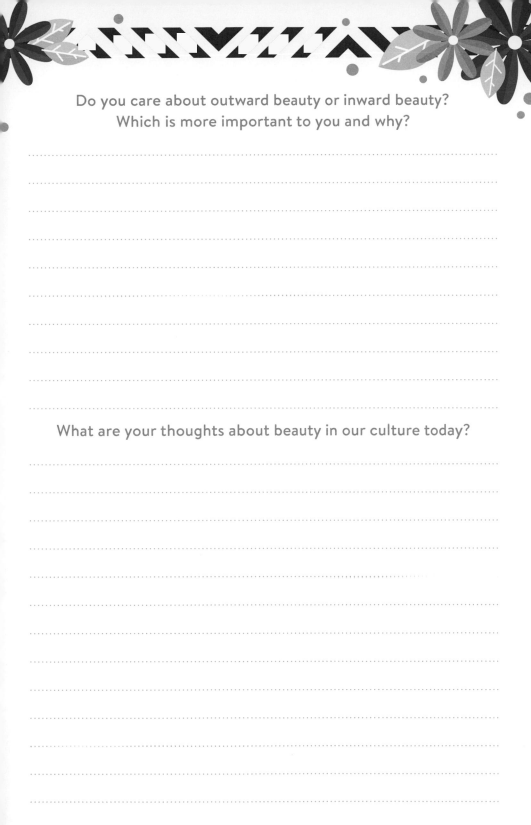

Do you care about outward beauty or inward beauty?
Which is more important to you and why?

What are your thoughts about beauty in our culture today?

How do you strive to keep the right perspective
about what true beauty is and is not?

# Section 4:

My faith is the *best* part of my story.

If you declare with your mouth, "Jesus is Lord," and believe in your heart that God raised him from the dead, you will be saved. For it is with your heart that you believe and are justified, and it is with your mouth that you profess your faith and are saved.

ROMANS 10:9–10 NIV

I became a Christian at .................................................... years old.

Describe your experience of accepting Jesus as Lord of your life.

In what ways has your faith grown since you became a Christian?

*But grow in the grace and knowledge of our Lord
and Savior Jesus Christ. To him be the glory
both now and to the day of eternity.*
2 PETER 3:18 ESV

Can others tell that you are a Christian? In what ways?
How do you live out your faith *and* share it with others?

_____

_____

_____

_____

_____

_____

_____

_____

_____

_____

_____

_____

_____

_____

_____

_____

_____

_____

_____

*Worship Christ as Lord of your life. And if*
*someone asks about your hope as a believer,*
*always be ready to explain it.*
1 PETER 3:15 NLT

How is the fruit of the Spirit evident in your life?

*But the fruit of the Spirit is love, joy, peace,
patience, kindness, goodness, faithfulness,
gentleness, self-control; against such
things there is no law.*
GALATIANS 5:22–23 ESV

Have any events or circumstances in your life
caused you to question your faith?

The name of my church is ..................................................................................

I love this church because ...............................................................................

.................................................................................................................

.................................................................................................................

.................................................................................................................

.................................................................................................................

.................................................................................................................

.................................................................................................................

.................................................................................................................

.................................................................................................................

.................................................................................................................

.................................................................................................................

.................................................................................................................

.................................................................................................................

.................................................................................................................

.................................................................................................................

.................................................................................................................

.................................................................................................................

.................................................................................................................

.................................................................................................................

*Let us hold unswervingly to the hope we profess, for he who promised
is faithful. And let us consider how we may spur one another on
toward love and good deeds, not giving up meeting together,
as some are in the habit of doing, but encouraging one another—
and all the more as you see the Day approaching.*
HEBREWS 10:23–25 NIV

The ways I give and serve and worship in this church are

*Serve the LORD with gladness!*
*Come into his presence with singing!*
PSALM 100:2 ESV

What are your spiritual gifts?
How are they evident in your life, and how do you use
them to bring glory to God and serve others?

*We have different gifts, according
to the grace given to each of us.*
ROMANS 12:6 NIV

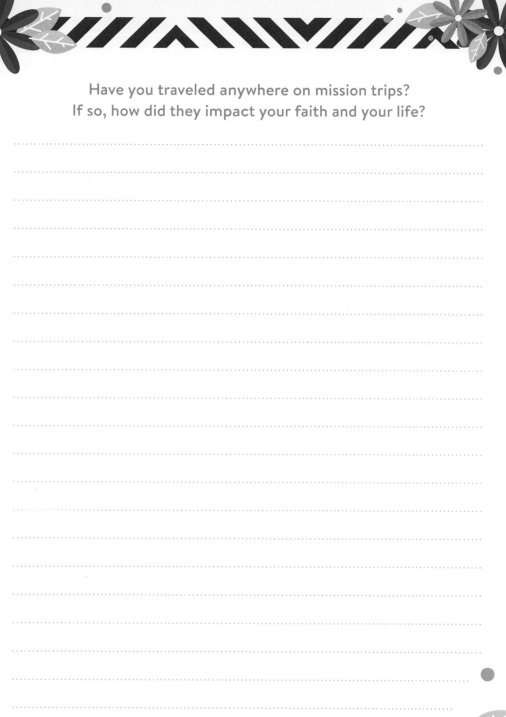

Have you traveled anywhere on mission trips?
If so, how did they impact your faith and your life?

*The Scriptures say, "How beautiful are the
feet of messengers who bring good news!"*
ROMANS 10:15 NLT

I feel closest to God when

*Jesus often withdrew to lonely
places and prayed.*
LUKE 5:16 NIV

I have experienced these miracles in my life:

*Your ways, God, are holy.*
*What god is as great as our God?*
*You are the God who performs miracles;*
*you display your power among the peoples.*
PSALM 77:13–14 NIV

43

My favorite scripture is ........................................................ ,

because .................................................................................

.................................................................................

.................................................................................

.................................................................................

.................................................................................

.................................................................................

.................................................................................

.................................................................................

My favorite worship song is ...................................... ,

because .................................................................................

.................................................................................

.................................................................................

.................................................................................

.................................................................................

.................................................................................

.................................................................................

.................................................................................

.................................................................................

.................................................................................

.................................................................................

My favorite ways and places to worship God are

Describe the ways you stay committed
to your faith in Jesus Christ.

........................................................................
........................................................................
........................................................................
........................................................................
........................................................................
........................................................................
........................................................................
........................................................................
........................................................................
........................................................................
........................................................................
........................................................................
........................................................................
........................................................................
........................................................................
........................................................................
........................................................................
........................................................................
........................................................................
........................................................................
........................................................................
........................................................................

*Cling to your faith in Christ,
and keep your conscience clear.*
1 TIMOTHY 1:19 NLT

# Section 5:

**My family is part of my story.**

Let love be genuine. Abhor what is evil; hold fast to what is good. Love one another with brotherly affection. Outdo one another in showing honor.

ROMANS 12:9–10 ESV

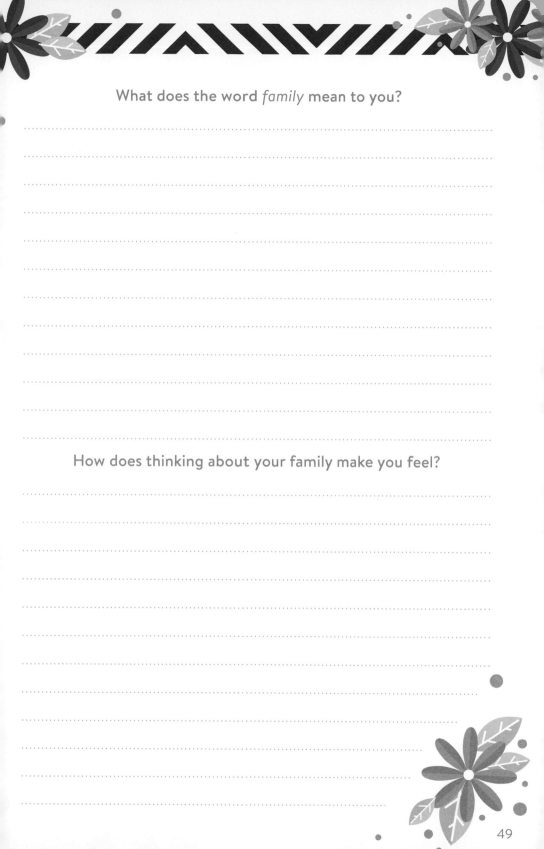

What does the word *family* mean to you?

How does thinking about your family make you feel?

These words best describe my mom:

My earliest memory of my mom is

I feel most loved by my mom when she

*Her children rise up and call her blessed.*
PROVERBS **31:28** ESV

I have conflict with my mom when

We work it out by

My favorite things to do with my mom are ........................................................

.............................................................................................................

.............................................................................................................

.............................................................................................................

.............................................................................................................

.............................................................................................................

.............................................................................................................

.............................................................................................................

.............................................................................................................

.............................................................................................................

.............................................................................................................

.............................................................................................................

My mom inspires me because ..................................................................

.............................................................................................................

.............................................................................................................

.............................................................................................................

.............................................................................................................

.............................................................................................................

.............................................................................................................

.............................................................................................................

.............................................................................................................

.............................................................................................................

.............................................................................................................

.............................................................................................................

The best advice my mom ever gave me is

*Don't neglect your
mother's instruction.*
PROVERBS 6:20 NLT

Describe how your relationship with your mom has developed and changed over the years.

These words best describe my dad:

What I love most about my dad is

I feel most loved by my dad when he

*As a father shows compassion to his
children, so the LORD shows compassion
to those who fear him.*
PSALM 103:13 ESV

I have conflict with my dad when ...........................................................

..........................................................................................................

..........................................................................................................

..........................................................................................................

..........................................................................................................

..........................................................................................................

..........................................................................................................

..........................................................................................................

..........................................................................................................

..........................................................................................................

We work it out by ...............................................................................

..........................................................................................................

..........................................................................................................

..........................................................................................................

..........................................................................................................

..........................................................................................................

..........................................................................................................

..........................................................................................................

..........................................................................................................

..........................................................................................................

My favorite things to do with my dad are

My dad inspires me because

The best advice my dad ever gave me is

*Listen to your father*
*who gave you life.*
Proverbs 23:22 esv

Describe how your relationship has changed
with your dad over the years.

I have ........................................ (number of) siblings.

Are your siblings older, younger, or both? ........................................

........................................................................

........................................................................

........................................................................

........................................................................

........................................................................

Describe your relationships with your siblings and
how birth order has affected your relationships.

........................................................................

........................................................................

........................................................................

........................................................................

........................................................................

........................................................................

........................................................................

........................................................................

........................................................................

........................................................................

........................................................................

........................................................................

........................................................................

........................................................................

My favorite ways to spend time with my siblings are .......................

..............................................................

..............................................................

..............................................................

..............................................................

..............................................................

..............................................................

..............................................................

..............................................................

..............................................................

..............................................................

What causes the most conflict with your siblings
and how do you work it out?

..............................................................

..............................................................

..............................................................

..............................................................

..............................................................

..............................................................

..............................................................

..............................................................

..............................................................

..............................................................

My siblings inspire and/or help me in these ways:

*Most important of all, continue to show
deep love for each other, for love
covers a multitude of sins.*
1 Peter 4:8 NLT

If you don't have siblings, do you wish you did?
Or are you happy being an only child?

My grandparents' names are ............................................................................................................

..........................................................................................................................................................

..........................................................................................................................................................

..........................................................................................................................................................

..........................................................................................................................................................

..........................................................................................................................................................

..........................................................................................................................................................

Describe your relationships with your grandparents.

..........................................................................................................................................................

..........................................................................................................................................................

..........................................................................................................................................................

..........................................................................................................................................................

..........................................................................................................................................................

..........................................................................................................................................................

..........................................................................................................................................................

..........................................................................................................................................................

..........................................................................................................................................................

..........................................................................................................................................................

..........................................................................................................................................................

..........................................................................................................................................................

..........................................................................................................................................................

..........................................................................................................................................................

..........................................................................................................................................................

What wisdom have you gained from your
relationships with your grandparents?

......................................................................................................
......................................................................................................
......................................................................................................
......................................................................................................
......................................................................................................
......................................................................................................
......................................................................................................
......................................................................................................
......................................................................................................
......................................................................................................
......................................................................................................
......................................................................................................
......................................................................................................
......................................................................................................
......................................................................................................
......................................................................................................
......................................................................................................
......................................................................................................
......................................................................................................

*Gray hair is a crown of glory;*
*it is gained in a righteous life.*
PROVERBS 16:31 ESV

Share a favorite activity you've enjoyed with grandparents.

Share a favorite memory you have with grandparents.

......................................................................................................................
......................................................................................................................
......................................................................................................................
......................................................................................................................
......................................................................................................................
......................................................................................................................
......................................................................................................................
......................................................................................................................
......................................................................................................................
......................................................................................................................
......................................................................................................................
......................................................................................................................
......................................................................................................................
......................................................................................................................
......................................................................................................................
......................................................................................................................
......................................................................................................................
......................................................................................................................
......................................................................................................................
......................................................................................................................

*Grandchildren are the crown of the aged,*
*and the glory of children is their fathers.*
PROVERBS 17:6 ESV

My closest aunts and uncles are

Describe your relationships with your aunts and uncles.

My favorite activities/memories with my aunts and uncles are

My closest cousins are ........................................................................................

........................................................................................

........................................................................................

........................................................................................

........................................................................................

........................................................................................

........................................................................................

........................................................................................

........................................................................................

........................................................................................

........................................................................................

Describe your relationships with your closest cousins.

........................................................................................

........................................................................................

........................................................................................

........................................................................................

........................................................................................

........................................................................................

........................................................................................

........................................................................................

........................................................................................

........................................................................................

My favorite activities/memories with my cousins are

Have you ever lost a family member?
How did you grieve their loss?
How do you honor their lives?

*"Blessed are those who mourn,*
*for they shall be comforted."*
MATTHEW 5:4 ESV

# Section 6:

My friends are part of my story.

Two people are better off than one, for they can help each other succeed. If one person falls, the other can reach out and help. But someone who falls alone is in real trouble. Likewise, two people lying close together can keep each other warm. But how can one be warm alone? A person standing alone can be attacked and defeated, but two can stand back-to-back and conquer. Three are even better, for a triple-braided cord is not easily broken.

ECCLESIASTES 4:9–12 NLT

Share favorite memories from your early childhood friendships.

*Therefore encourage one another and build
one another up, just as you are doing.*
1 THESSALONIANS 5:11 ESV

One of my closest friends today is .....................................................................

..................................................................................................................

Describe your friendship. What connected you in the beginning and what keeps you connected today?

..................................................................................................................
..................................................................................................................
..................................................................................................................
..................................................................................................................
..................................................................................................................
..................................................................................................................
..................................................................................................................
..................................................................................................................
..................................................................................................................
..................................................................................................................
..................................................................................................................
..................................................................................................................
..................................................................................................................
..................................................................................................................
..................................................................................................................
..................................................................................................................
..................................................................................................................
..................................................................................................................
..................................................................................................................
..................................................................................................................

Another of my closest friends is ............................................................................

.......................................................................................................................................

Describe your friendship. What connected you in the
beginning and what keeps you connected today?

Yet another of my closest friends is ..................................................................
..............................................................................................................................

### Describe your friendship. What connected you in the beginning and what keeps you connected today?

..............................................................................................................................

..............................................................................................................................

..............................................................................................................................

..............................................................................................................................

..............................................................................................................................

..............................................................................................................................

..............................................................................................................................

..............................................................................................................................

..............................................................................................................................

..............................................................................................................................

..............................................................................................................................

..............................................................................................................................

..............................................................................................................................

..............................................................................................................................

..............................................................................................................................

..............................................................................................................................

..............................................................................................................................

..............................................................................................................................

..............................................................................................................................

..............................................................................................................................

Describe a perfect day hanging out with your friends.

How much do you use social media to
develop and maintain friendships?
What are the benefits and dangers of
social media for your friendships?

Describe the difference between real friends
and social media "friends" and "followers."

Do you behave online the same as you do in real life? Explain.

Share an experience of when a friendship ended.
What did you learn from that experience?

Have you experienced the death of a friend? How did you grieve the loss? How do you honor the life of that friend now?

What qualities make a good friend? Do you feel like you are a good friend to others?

*As iron sharpens iron,*
*so a friend sharpens a friend.*
PROVERBS 27:17 NLT

What challenges are there in maintaining great friendships?

............................................................................

............................................................................

............................................................................

............................................................................

............................................................................

............................................................................

............................................................................

............................................................................

............................................................................

............................................................................

............................................................................

............................................................................

............................................................................

............................................................................

............................................................................

............................................................................

............................................................................

............................................................................

............................................................................

............................................................................

*A friend loves at all times.*
PROVERBS 17:17 NIV

# Section 7:

My education is part of my story.

*Fear of the LORD is the foundation of true knowledge, but fools despise wisdom and discipline.*

**PROVERBS 1:7** NLT

The school I currently attend is ...........................................................................

I am in ................................................................................................... grade.

My past schools were ......................................................................................

..............................................................................................................

My school mascot is ........................................................................................

School makes me feel .......................................................................................

...............................................................................................................

...............................................................................................................

...............................................................................................................

...............................................................................................................

...............................................................................................................

...............................................................................................................

...............................................................................................................

...............................................................................................................

...............................................................................................................

...............................................................................................................

...............................................................................................................

...............................................................................................................

...............................................................................................................

...............................................................................................................

...............................................................................................................

...............................................................................................................

*For the LORD gives wisdom; from his mouth
come knowledge and understanding.*

PROVERBS 2:6 ESV

What time does your school day begin?
What time does it end?
How do you feel about these times?

Describe your typical school-day schedule.

My favorite subjects in elementary school were ....................................
.................................................... because ....................................

....................................................................................................

....................................................................................................

....................................................................................................

....................................................................................................

....................................................................................................

....................................................................................................

....................................................................................................

....................................................................................................

My favorite teachers in elementary school were ....................................
.................................................... because ....................................

....................................................................................................

....................................................................................................

....................................................................................................

....................................................................................................

....................................................................................................

....................................................................................................

....................................................................................................

....................................................................................................

....................................................................................................

....................................................................................................

....................................................................................................

Describe the subjects and teachers you struggled with the most in elementary school and why.

Describe a favorite memory from elementary school.

My current favorite subject is ..........................................................................................................
.......................................................... because ..............................................................
...........................................................................................................................................
...........................................................................................................................................
...........................................................................................................................................
...........................................................................................................................................
...........................................................................................................................................
...........................................................................................................................................
...........................................................................................................................................
...........................................................................................................................................
...........................................................................................................................................

My current favorite teachers are ......................................................................................................
.......................................................... because ..............................................................
...........................................................................................................................................
...........................................................................................................................................
...........................................................................................................................................
...........................................................................................................................................
...........................................................................................................................................
...........................................................................................................................................
...........................................................................................................................................
...........................................................................................................................................
...........................................................................................................................................
...........................................................................................................................................
...........................................................................................................................................

Describe the subjects and teachers you
struggle with the most and why.

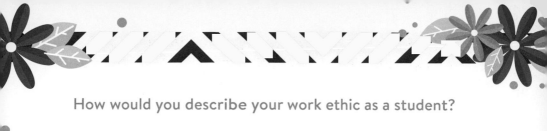

How would you describe your work ethic as a student?

..............................................................................................................

..............................................................................................................

..............................................................................................................

..............................................................................................................

..............................................................................................................

..............................................................................................................

..............................................................................................................

..............................................................................................................

How would your parents and teachers describe
your work ethic as a student?

..............................................................................................................

..............................................................................................................

..............................................................................................................

..............................................................................................................

..............................................................................................................

..............................................................................................................

..............................................................................................................

..............................................................................................................

..............................................................................................................

*Work willingly at whatever you do, as though you were
working for the Lord rather than for people. Remember that
the Lord will give you an inheritance as your reward,
and that the Master you are serving is Christ.*
COLOSSIANS 3:23–24 NLT

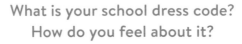

## What is your school dress code?
## How do you feel about it?

How do you feel when you work in a group to complete a project?

Describe your greatest accomplishment in school.
How did it make you feel to reach your goal?

Describe your favorite school lunch.

List all the things in your backpack on a typical day of school:

......................................................................................................
......................................................................................................
......................................................................................................
......................................................................................................
......................................................................................................
......................................................................................................
......................................................................................................
......................................................................................................
......................................................................................................
......................................................................................................
......................................................................................................
......................................................................................................

List all the things in your locker on a typical day of school:

......................................................................................................
......................................................................................................
......................................................................................................
......................................................................................................
......................................................................................................
......................................................................................................
......................................................................................................
......................................................................................................
......................................................................................................

What's the funniest thing you've ever experienced at school?

Share a memory of a favorite field trip or assembly.

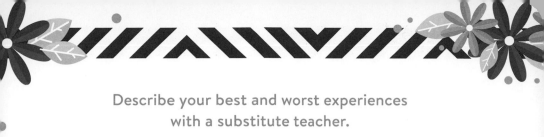

Describe your best and worst experiences
with a substitute teacher.

.................................................................................................

.................................................................................................

.................................................................................................

.................................................................................................

.................................................................................................

.................................................................................................

.................................................................................................

.................................................................................................

.................................................................................................

.................................................................................................

.................................................................................................

.................................................................................................

.................................................................................................

.................................................................................................

.................................................................................................

.................................................................................................

.................................................................................................

.................................................................................................

.................................................................................................

.................................................................................................

.................................................................................................

.................................................................................................

What are your favorite things to do during school breaks?

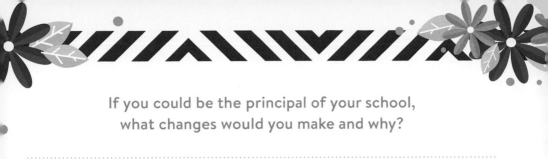

If you could be the principal of your school,
what changes would you make and why?

If you have an after-school or summer job, share about it here. What do you like and dislike about it?

Do you plan to attend college? Why or why not?

........................................................................................

........................................................................................

........................................................................................

........................................................................................

........................................................................................

........................................................................................

........................................................................................

If so, where would you like to attend?

........................................................................................

........................................................................................

What will you study?

........................................................................................

........................................................................................

Describe your hopes and dreams for your college experience.

........................................................................................

........................................................................................

........................................................................................

........................................................................................

........................................................................................

........................................................................................

........................................................................................

........................................................................................

Describe your dream job after graduating college.

If you don't plan to attend college, describe your plans
and goals for after high school graduation.

Write a prayer asking God for wisdom and direction
regarding your education and career.

# Section 8:

My activities and interests
are part of my story.

Delight yourself in the LORD,
and he will give you the
desires of your heart.

**PSALM 37:4** ESV

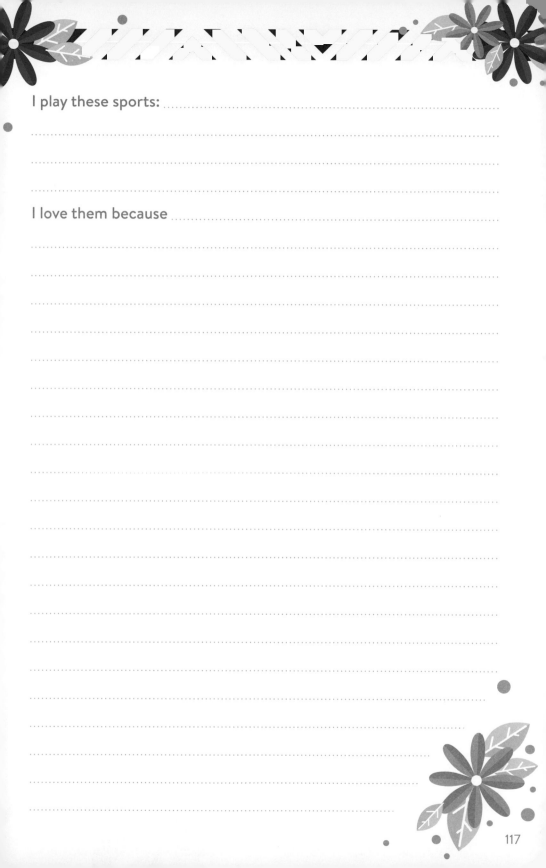

I play these sports: ...................................................................................................
...................................................................................................
...................................................................................................
...................................................................................................

I love them because ...............................................................................
...................................................................................................
...................................................................................................
...................................................................................................
...................................................................................................
...................................................................................................
...................................................................................................
...................................................................................................
...................................................................................................
...................................................................................................
...................................................................................................
...................................................................................................
...................................................................................................
...................................................................................................
...................................................................................................
...................................................................................................
...................................................................................................
...................................................................................................
...................................................................................................
...................................................................................................

I play these musical instruments:

I love them because

I'm involved in the following clubs or groups at school: ...................................

.......................................................................................................................

.......................................................................................................................

.......................................................................................................................

I love them because ....................................................................................

.......................................................................................................................

.......................................................................................................................

.......................................................................................................................

.......................................................................................................................

.......................................................................................................................

.......................................................................................................................

.......................................................................................................................

.......................................................................................................................

.......................................................................................................................

.......................................................................................................................

.......................................................................................................................

.......................................................................................................................

.......................................................................................................................

.......................................................................................................................

.......................................................................................................................

.......................................................................................................................

.......................................................................................................................

.......................................................................................................................

.......................................................................................................................

.......................................................................................................................

My hobbies are

How did you first become interested in these activities?

My favorite extracurricular activity is ............................................................
........................................................................................................................
........................................................................................................................
........................................................................................................................

because ...............................................................................................................
........................................................................................................................
........................................................................................................................
........................................................................................................................
........................................................................................................................
........................................................................................................................
........................................................................................................................
........................................................................................................................
........................................................................................................................
........................................................................................................................
........................................................................................................................
........................................................................................................................
........................................................................................................................
........................................................................................................................
........................................................................................................................
........................................................................................................................
........................................................................................................................
........................................................................................................................
........................................................................................................................
........................................................................................................................

List the pets you have now or have had in the past.

Describe your favorite things about each pet.

Do you love to travel? Why or why not?

Do you frequently travel to the same places? . . .
Or do you like to experience a different
place each time you travel?

## List all the places you have traveled to.

Do you prefer road trips or flights? Why? ....................................................

......................................................................................................

......................................................................................................

......................................................................................................

......................................................................................................

......................................................................................................

......................................................................................................

......................................................................................................

......................................................................................................

......................................................................................................

......................................................................................................

......................................................................................................

......................................................................................................

......................................................................................................

......................................................................................................

......................................................................................................

......................................................................................................

*Look here, you who say, "Today or tomorrow we are going to
a certain town and will stay there a year. We will do business
there and make a profit." How do you know what your
life will be like tomorrow? Your life is like the morning
fog—it's here a little while, then it's gone. What you
ought to say is, "If the Lord wants us to,
we will live and do this or that."*
JAMES 4:13–15 NLT

If your budget had no limit, where would you
travel for vacation and why?

List your favorite books. Describe why they
are so meaningful to you.

List your favorite kinds of music and musicians.
Describe what you like best about each.

........................................................................
........................................................................
........................................................................
........................................................................
........................................................................
........................................................................
........................................................................
........................................................................
........................................................................
........................................................................
........................................................................
........................................................................
........................................................................
........................................................................
........................................................................
........................................................................
........................................................................
........................................................................
........................................................................

*Oh come, let us sing to the LORD;*
*let us make a joyful noise to the*
*rock of our salvation!*
PSALM 95:1 ESV

List your favorite TV shows and movies.
What do you enjoy most about them?

## Shopping? Thumbs up or thumbs down and why?

I ........................................... (do or do not) like to cook because

..........................................................................................

..........................................................................................

..........................................................................................

..........................................................................................

..........................................................................................

..........................................................................................

..........................................................................................

..........................................................................................

My favorite foods are .................................................................

..........................................................................................

..........................................................................................

..........................................................................................

..........................................................................................

..........................................................................................

..........................................................................................

..........................................................................................

My favorite restaurants are ..........................................................

..........................................................................................

..........................................................................................

..........................................................................................

..........................................................................................

..........................................................................................

..........................................................................................

..........................................................................................

My least favorite foods are

My least favorite restaurants are

........................................................... always makes me smile.

........................................................... always makes me laugh.

........................................................... always makes me cry.

........................................................... always makes me angry.

........................................................... always frustrates me.

........................................................... always bores me.

........................................................... always excites me.

........................................................... always exhausts me.

........................................................... always energizes me.

..................................................................................................

..................................................................................................

..................................................................................................

..................................................................................................

..................................................................................................

..................................................................................................

..................................................................................................

..................................................................................................

..................................................................................................

..................................................................................................

..................................................................................................

..................................................................................................

*There is a time for everything, and a season for
every activity under the heavens. . .a time to
weep and a time to laugh, a time to
mourn and a time to dance.*
ECCLESIASTES 3:1, 4 NIV

My favorite board games to play are ..................................................
..................................................................................................

My favorite crafty thing to do is ..................................................
..................................................................................................

My favorite social media site is ..................................................
..................................................................................................

My favorite news source is ..................................................
..................................................................................................

My favorite magazine is ..................................................
..................................................................................................

My favorite emoji is ..................................................
..................................................................................................

My favorite thing to do on a rainy day is ..................................................
..................................................................................................
..................................................................................................

My favorite thing to do on a sunny day is ..................................................
..................................................................................................
..................................................................................................

Do you follow the news and current events?
Why or why not?

If you could break a world record, what would it be and why?

Describe your pet peeves. Why do they annoy you so much?

Do you prefer to be outdoors or indoors?

What are your favorite outdoor activities?

What are your favorite indoor activities?

My favorite way to exercise is ................................................................................

...........................................................................................................................

...........................................................................................................................

...........................................................................................................................

...........................................................................................................................

...........................................................................................................................

...........................................................................................................................

...........................................................................................................................

...........................................................................................................................

Are you doing a good job taking care of your health, or do you need to make major improvements? How could you improve?

...........................................................................................................................

...........................................................................................................................

...........................................................................................................................

...........................................................................................................................

...........................................................................................................................

...........................................................................................................................

...........................................................................................................................

...........................................................................................................................

...........................................................................................................................

...........................................................................................................................

*For physical training is of some value,
but godliness has value for all things,
holding promise for both the present
life and the life to come.*
1 TIMOTHY 4:8 NIV

What I love most about Easter is

Describe your family traditions for this holiday.

What I love most about the Fourth of July is ........................................

........................................................................................................................

........................................................................................................................

........................................................................................................................

........................................................................................................................

........................................................................................................................

........................................................................................................................

........................................................................................................................

........................................................................................................................

........................................................................................................................

Describe your family traditions for this holiday.

........................................................................................................................

........................................................................................................................

........................................................................................................................

........................................................................................................................

........................................................................................................................

........................................................................................................................

........................................................................................................................

........................................................................................................................

........................................................................................................................

........................................................................................................................

........................................................................................................................

........................................................................................................................

What I love most about Thanksgiving is

Describe your family traditions for this holiday.

What I love most about Christmas is

Describe your family traditions for this holiday.

What I love most about New Year's Eve is ..............................................
................................................................................................
................................................................................................
................................................................................................
................................................................................................
................................................................................................
................................................................................................
................................................................................................
................................................................................................

Describe your family traditions for this holiday.

................................................................................................
................................................................................................
................................................................................................
................................................................................................
................................................................................................
................................................................................................
................................................................................................
................................................................................................
................................................................................................
................................................................................................

Do you make a big deal about birthdays—either yours or others'? How do you like to celebrate?

........................................................................
........................................................................
........................................................................
........................................................................
........................................................................
........................................................................
........................................................................
........................................................................
........................................................................
........................................................................
........................................................................
........................................................................
........................................................................
........................................................................
........................................................................
........................................................................
........................................................................
........................................................................
........................................................................
........................................................................

*"The Lord bless you and keep you; the Lord make his face shine on you and be gracious to you; the Lord turn his face toward you and give you peace."*
NUMBERS 6:24–26 NIV

Share a memory of a favorite birthday celebration.

My favorite season of the year is ................................................
because ................................................

<br>

For everything there is a season,
and a time for every matter under heaven.
ECCLESIASTES 3:1 ESV

What I love about winter is .................................................................................................
.......................................................................................................................................
.......................................................................................................................................
.......................................................................................................................................
.......................................................................................................................................
.......................................................................................................................................
.......................................................................................................................................
.......................................................................................................................................
.......................................................................................................................................

What I don't love about winter is ......................................................................................
.......................................................................................................................................
.......................................................................................................................................
.......................................................................................................................................
.......................................................................................................................................
.......................................................................................................................................
.......................................................................................................................................
.......................................................................................................................................
.......................................................................................................................................
.......................................................................................................................................

What I love about spring is

What I don't love about spring is

What I love about summer is

What I don't love about summer is

What I love about fall is ................................................................................

.......................................................................................................

.......................................................................................................

.......................................................................................................

.......................................................................................................

.......................................................................................................

.......................................................................................................

.......................................................................................................

.......................................................................................................

.......................................................................................................

.......................................................................................................

.......................................................................................................

.......................................................................................................

What I don't love about fall is ................................................................

...........       .....................................................................................

.......................................................................................................

.......................................................................................................

.......................................................................................................

.......................................................................................................

.......................................................................................................

.......................................................................................................

.......................................................................................................

.......................................................................................................

.......................................................................................................

.......................................................................................................

.......................................................................................................

Describe the best gift you've ever received.
Who gave it to you? Was it for a special occasion?

*Every good gift and every perfect gift is from above,*
*coming down from the Father of lights,*
*with whom there is no variation*
*or shadow due to change.*
JAMES 1:17 ESV

# Section 9:

My role models are part of my story.

And you should imitate me,
just as I imitate Christ.

**1 Corinthians 11:1** nlt

What special qualities make a person role model–worthy?

List the teachers, leaders, mentors, and coaches in your life
who made a huge impact on you. How have they
helped change your life for the better?

*When we get together, I want to*
*encourage you in your faith,*
*but I also want to be*
*encouraged by yours.*
ROMANS 1:12 NLT

List any modern-day celebrities whom you admire and why.

I am most inspired by these Christian heroes of the faith:

*By faith these people overthrew
kingdoms, ruled with justice,
and received what God
had promised them.*
HEBREWS 11:33 NLT

Share about the people you are most looking
forward to meeting or seeing again in heaven.

How do you keep this proper perspective: all human role models will likely fail. . .and only Jesus Christ is your perfect example?

_Imitate God, therefore, in everything you do, because you are his dear children. Live a life filled with love, following the example of Christ. He loved us and offered himself as a sacrifice for us, a pleasing aroma to God._

EPHESIANS 5:1–2 NLT

# Section 10:

**The places I've lived are part of my story.**

"The God who made the world and everything in it is the Lord of heaven and earth and does not live in temples built by human hands. . . . From one man he made all the nations, that they should inhabit the whole earth; and he marked out their appointed times in history and the boundaries of their lands. . . . 'For in [God] we live and move and have our being.'"

ACTS 17:24, 26, 28 NIV

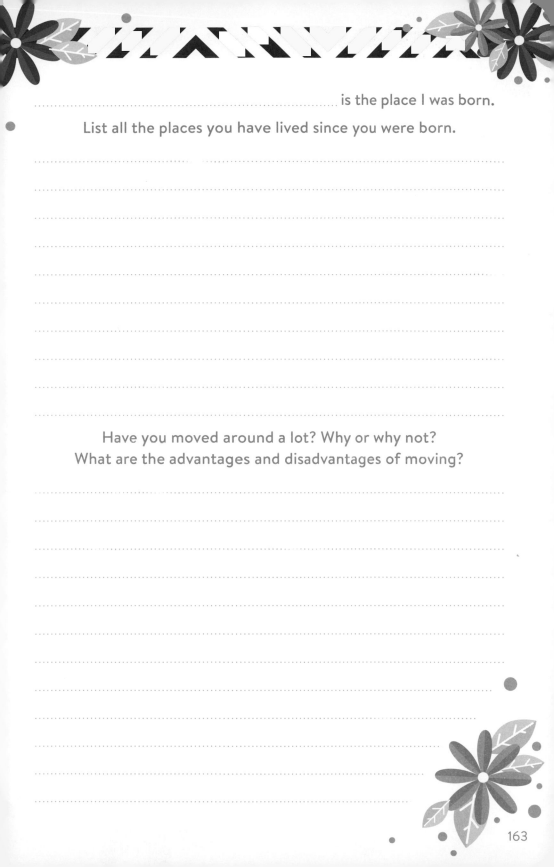

.................................................................................................... is the place I was born.

List all the places you have lived since you were born.

Have you moved around a lot? Why or why not?
What are the advantages and disadvantages of moving?

Describe the house you currently live in.

How does your bedroom look right now?
What is your decorating style? Are you messy or neat?

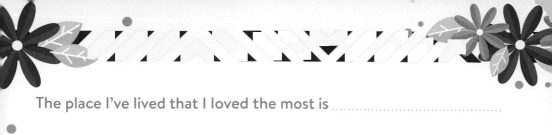

The place I've lived that I loved the most is

Why?

The place I've lived that I disliked the most is ..............................................
Why? ............................................................................................................

..............................................................................................................................

..............................................................................................................................

..............................................................................................................................

..............................................................................................................................

..............................................................................................................................

..............................................................................................................................

..............................................................................................................................

..............................................................................................................................

..............................................................................................................................

..............................................................................................................................

..............................................................................................................................

..............................................................................................................................

..............................................................................................................................

..............................................................................................................................

..............................................................................................................................

..............................................................................................................................

..............................................................................................................................

..............................................................................................................................

..............................................................................................................................

..............................................................................................................................

How have the different places you've lived helped
to develop you into the person you are?

..........................................................................................................
..........................................................................................................
..........................................................................................................
..........................................................................................................
..........................................................................................................
..........................................................................................................
..........................................................................................................
..........................................................................................................
..........................................................................................................
..........................................................................................................

How will the places you live continue to develop you in the future?

..........................................................................................................
..........................................................................................................
..........................................................................................................
..........................................................................................................
..........................................................................................................
..........................................................................................................
..........................................................................................................
..........................................................................................................
..........................................................................................................
..........................................................................................................

My dream home for my family would be ...............................................
..............................................................................
..............................................................................
..............................................................................
..............................................................................
..............................................................................
..............................................................................
..............................................................................

It would have these features: ...............................................
..............................................................................
..............................................................................
..............................................................................
..............................................................................
..............................................................................
..............................................................................
..............................................................................
..............................................................................
..............................................................................
..............................................................................
..............................................................................
..............................................................................

# Section 11:

My struggles and triumphs
are part of my story.

Three different times I begged the Lord to take it away. Each time he said, "My grace is all you need. My power works best in weakness." So now I am glad to boast about my weaknesses, so that the power of Christ can work through me. That's why I take pleasure in my weaknesses, and in the insults, hardships, persecutions, and troubles that I suffer for Christ. For when I am weak, then I am strong.

2 CORINTHIANS 12:8–10 NLT

This is what stresses me out the most in life: ........................................

..............................................................................................

..............................................................................................

..............................................................................................

..............................................................................................

..............................................................................................

..............................................................................................

..............................................................................................

..............................................................................................

Describe how you take care of yourself
after an extremely stressful day.

..............................................................................................

..............................................................................................

..............................................................................................

..............................................................................................

..............................................................................................

..............................................................................................

..............................................................................................

..............................................................................................

..............................................................................................

..............................................................................................

..............................................................................................

*Cast all your anxiety on him*
*because he cares for you.*
1 PETER 5:7 NIV

I've had these major illnesses and injuries in my life:

I have had these surgeries in my life:

How did God carry you through your health problems?
What did you learn from these experiences?

The worst trials and hardships I have experienced are

How did God strengthen and help you through these hard things?
What did He teach you that you would never
have learned otherwise?

Share your "most embarrassing moment" story.

........................................................................................
........................................................................................
........................................................................................
........................................................................................
........................................................................................
........................................................................................
........................................................................................
........................................................................................
........................................................................................
........................................................................................
........................................................................................
........................................................................................
........................................................................................
........................................................................................
........................................................................................
........................................................................................
........................................................................................

*Dear brothers and sisters, when troubles of any kind come your way, consider it an opportunity for great joy. For you know that when your faith is tested, your endurance has a chance to grow. So let it grow, for when your endurance is fully developed, you will be perfect and complete, needing nothing.*
JAMES 1:2–4 NLT

Describe the worst mistake you've ever made.

.......................................................................................

.......................................................................................

.......................................................................................

.......................................................................................

.......................................................................................

.......................................................................................

.......................................................................................

How did it get resolved? How did God help you through it?
What did you learn from it?

.......................................................................................

.......................................................................................

.......................................................................................

.......................................................................................

.......................................................................................

.......................................................................................

.......................................................................................

.......................................................................................

*If we confess our sins, he is faithful and just to
forgive us our sins and to cleanse us
from all unrighteousness.*
1 JOHN 1:9 ESV

## What are your deepest fears?

......................................................................................

......................................................................................

......................................................................................

......................................................................................

......................................................................................

......................................................................................

## What causes you the most anxiety?

......................................................................................

......................................................................................

......................................................................................

......................................................................................

......................................................................................

......................................................................................

## In what ways do you strive to give *all* your worries over to God and let His peace rule over you?

......................................................................................

......................................................................................

......................................................................................

......................................................................................

......................................................................................

......................................................................................

# Section 12:

My dreams for marriage and
family are part of my story.

Let marriage be held in
honor among all.

HEBREWS 13:4 ESV

Love bears all things, believes all things,
hopes all things, endures all things.

1 CORINTHIANS 13:7 ESV

Do you hope to get married someday? Why or why not?

What qualities are important to look for in a husband?

Write a prayer asking God to bless and prepare both
you and your future husband for marriage.

Describe a perfect first date.

Describe what the perfect engagement ring would look like.

...................................................................................................
...................................................................................................
...................................................................................................
...................................................................................................
...................................................................................................
...................................................................................................
...................................................................................................

Describe what the perfect engagement story would be.

...................................................................................................
...................................................................................................
...................................................................................................
...................................................................................................
...................................................................................................
...................................................................................................
...................................................................................................
...................................................................................................
...................................................................................................
...................................................................................................
...................................................................................................

*For as a young man marries a young woman,*
*so shall your sons marry you, and as the*
*bridegroom rejoices over the bride,*
*so shall your God rejoice over you.*
ISAIAH 62:5 ESV

My dream wedding dress would look like ...........................................................
...................................................................................................................
...................................................................................................................
...................................................................................................................
...................................................................................................................

My dream wedding decor would be ...............................................................
...................................................................................................................
...................................................................................................................
...................................................................................................................
...................................................................................................................

My dream wedding location would be ...........................................................
...................................................................................................................
...................................................................................................................
...................................................................................................................
...................................................................................................................

My dream wedding ceremony would be .........................................................
...................................................................................................................
...................................................................................................................
...................................................................................................................
...................................................................................................................
...................................................................................................................
...................................................................................................................

If you picked your wedding party right now,
who would be in it and why?

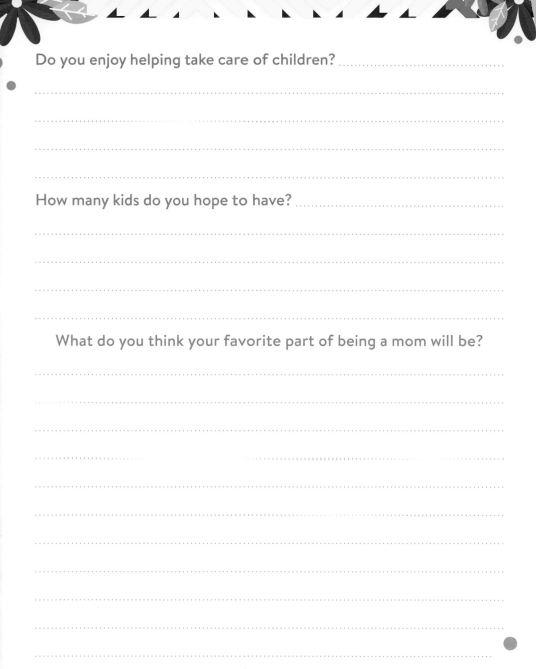

Do you enjoy helping take care of children? .......................................................

..........................................................................................................................

..........................................................................................................................

..........................................................................................................................

..........................................................................................................................

How many kids do you hope to have? ...............................................................

..........................................................................................................................

..........................................................................................................................

..........................................................................................................................

What do you think your favorite part of being a mom will be?

..........................................................................................................................

..........................................................................................................................

..........................................................................................................................

..........................................................................................................................

..........................................................................................................................

..........................................................................................................................

..........................................................................................................................

..........................................................................................................................

..........................................................................................................................

*Children are a gift from the L*ORD*;*
*they are a reward from him.*
PSALM 127:3 NLT

What do you think will be the most difficult/
challenging part of being a mom?

How do you think your parenting style will be similar to or different from the way you have been raised?

........................................................................................................
........................................................................................................
........................................................................................................
........................................................................................................
........................................................................................................
........................................................................................................
........................................................................................................
........................................................................................................
........................................................................................................
........................................................................................................
........................................................................................................
........................................................................................................
........................................................................................................
........................................................................................................
........................................................................................................
........................................................................................................
........................................................................................................
........................................................................................................
........................................................................................................
........................................................................................................
........................................................................................................

*Direct your children onto the right path,*
*and when they are older, they will not leave it.*
PROVERBS 22:6 NLT

Write a prayer asking God to guide and
direct your hopes and dreams for a family.

# Section 13:

God will continue to work in my
life. . .for *all* my days.

Being confident of this, that he who began a good work in you will carry it on to completion until the day of Christ Jesus.

God is still helping to write the story of me.
Here is how I want my story to continue. . .

# Continue Your Faith Journey!

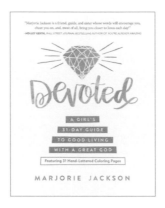

## *Devoted*

Young women are invited to join author Marjorie Jackson in *Devoted*, a 31-day devotional about letting love and dedication to Jesus penetrate every area of life. Whether you're a long-time Christian or if your spiritual training wheels are still on, this book will help you dive into God's Word and discover what it truly means to be a young woman who is *completely*, *joyfully*, *beautifully* different.

Paperback / 978-1-68322-166-1 / $12.99

Find This and More from Barbour
Publishing at Your Favorite Bookstore
or at www.barbourbooks.com